A Beanie and a Cup of Tea

A Beanie and a Cup of Tea

A Father's Poems of Loss and Love

Larry A. Dunn

RESOURCE *Publications* · Eugene, Oregon

A BEANIE AND A CUP OF TEA
A Father's Poems of Loss and Love

Resource Publications
An Imprint of Wipf and Stock Publishers
199 W. 8th Ave., Suite 3
Eugene, OR 97401

www.wipfandstock.com

PAPERBACK ISBN: 978-1-6667-1586-6
HARDCOVER ISBN: 978-1-6667-1587-3
EBOOK ISBN: 978-1-6667-1588-0

.   OCTOBER 27, 2021 3:41 PM

Permission granted by Jean Janzen for use of the poem, "Original Blessing."

To Jean, who saw the beauty of love in words of sorrow.

Certain realities in life can only be seen through eyes cleansed by tears.

—POPE FRANCIS

Contents

II.

III.

Preface

SHORTLY AFTER MY SON Seth's death on August 1, 2011, I discovered a gift he gave me. It was the gift of poetry. I don't mean that I found a poem Seth had written, or learned that poetry was an interest of his previously unknown to me. Rather, I mean that I started doing something I had never done before—writing poems that arose from my loss and love for my son.

As an academic, I had written various forms of prose for years and was in the middle of completing my first book when this tragic event struck our lives. I was an author but never imagined myself a poet. I couldn't even recall having taken a course in poetry in all my years of study!

My first poem, consisting of four short lines, was a lament for my faith, questioning the significance of years of prayer for my sons and their future, which now seemed so vulnerable and uncertain.

My second poem, written three months later, was surprisingly accepting of Seth's death and more hopeful about how his memory would live on. Taking the form of a haiku, I still did not think of what I was writing as poetry, though I could see how the sparse words spoke honestly to the truth of my grief and how the empty spaces so powerfully expressed the sorrow and pain I felt.

Then Juan Felipe Herrera spoke at my university about his journey from son of a migrant farm worker to Poet Laureate of the United States. Felipe Herrera began his presentation as if speaking directly to me: "Don't think that poems are not poems," he said. "That's not what we do. Just write it, and read it, and share it with one other person." With these words, my heart opened to this unexpected gift, and I immediately began writing more frequently, often in the middle of the night awakened by a dream or thought of my son, pen in hand scribbling through tears.

At the same time, I was preparing to submit a proposal for my second sabbatical for which I was developing several ideas for research and writing projects. When I initially presented them to my dean, he recognized my passion around a more personal second book project I had included related to grief, expanding on some earlier writing I had done.

Taking a small risk on a senior faculty member, he expressed support for the project, which I had listed below other more "scholarly" ones within my academic discipline. Encouraged by his support and aware of similar works published by other scholars, I submitted my sabbatical proposal and it was approved.

With publication now in mind, I began to think about my writing as more than just personal grief work and focused on improving the quality of my poems. I asked my friend Jean Janzen, an accomplished and celebrated Fresno poet who is generous with her time and a kind soul who had known Seth through our involvement at church, if she would look at what I was writing. Jean graciously read my rough poems and offered to be my mentor, as she has been for so many. She simply saw it as being my friend. So, on a foggy January day in Fresno, we started meeting on a regular basis when my sabbatical semester began.

Patient and wise, Jean critically yet gently helped me to find truth and beauty in this unexpected gift. On occasion, my poems helped us to see how similar her grief journey was to mine in losing a dear husband and, tragically, a grandson in the time since Seth's death. As we drank tea and looked out to the garden through her kitchen window where we regularly met, marveling at the latest transformation of flowers and other plants, Jean and I walked together through the heartache and comfort of shared grief one poem at a time.

In the first days following Seth's death, a close friend wrote, "The only conclusion one can come to about the loss of a child is that it is an awful way to learn so little." To me, this gift is not part of some lesson or moral about what's to be gained or learned from the death of a child. I have no interest in that. Nor do I see it as a sign that I've arrived at a final destination on my journey of grief, or a "reason" for my loss, as some might suggest. No gift of any kind can make such a tragedy worthwhile—or even better, really. Gifts are rarely asked for; they're just given. We're taught to accept even unwanted ones graciously.

I have come to see Seth at the heart of this gift, nurtured with love and patience by those who have walked this difficult path with me. Out of that, I have learned how to walk alongside others who grieve losses, great and small. And I have learned a thing or two about poetry, and myself, through it.

❀ ❀ ❀

When my dear friend Christine read an early draft of this collection, she noted that it might require a bright orange sign like those warning motorists of approaching road construction. Perhaps, she suggested, it ought to announce: Grief Work Ahead! Indeed, the reader should be warned that these poems unapologetically refuse to look away from, sidestep, avoid, or deny the anguish that comes from the death of a child. I offer an honest and candid portrayal of what it means to sit with the pain of one's own loss while extending a knowing embrace around those whose lives are irrevocably shaped by grief.

I wrote this book primarily for those who need to know that someone understands the heartache and confusion of grief, without trying to "fix" it. It is strangely comforting to know you are not alone, even in the experience of something you would want no one else to share. These poems give permission to those who grieve to let the waves of emotions come without judgment, moving not around but through them as unflinchingly as possible. I hope that those grieving the death of a loved one, whether for a month or a decade, will recognize something from their own experience and in that find encouragement to carry on.

I also hope to balance the many voices of those trying to help people who grieve to feel better without being willing to bear or even acknowledge an ounce of their pain. That may just be a way of avoiding their own discomfort over the nightmare they see us living. But for the grieving, it can be painfully dismissive, hurtful, and isolating to be told that "everything will be alright." There are times when such feelings are almost unbearable, but the sorrow that comes from losing my son is also a connection to my continuing love for him and I wouldn't have it any other way.

Consequently, I haven't set out to give this collection the predictable but empty assurance of a healing arc, where the early poems of agony and grief inevitably give way to "finding peace," "acceptance," or "closure." That would suggest an ordering of that which can never be ordered, or allow that such ideas even make sense, at least in some predictable way. I simply don't want to amplify the "you'll get better" message that can be found almost anywhere. Some may want that, but by and large it won't be found here. Poetry doesn't only comfort the tortured soul; it gives voice to it.

With that, I now entrust the words on these pages—drawn from my personal well of sorrow—to you.

I.

My Apologies

I realize,
dear reader,
that you've had
nothing at all
to do with
any of this.

Until now.

Two Things (for Jean)

My mentor,
patient and wise,
told me that
all poetry
is about
just two things—
love and loss.

Well, I told her,
that is good
because
that is all I know.

FYI

Nobody wants to read
a whole goddamn book
of tears, grief,
sadness and pain,
suffering, loss,
dark clouds and rain—
page after page
of sorrow, despair,
mourning and heartache
beyond all compare.

Nobody wants to write it either.

Suddenly, a Beach House

Suddenly, a beach house
Suddenly, a hill
Suddenly, a skateboard
Suddenly, so still.

Suddenly, late summer fun
Suddenly, a fall
Suddenly, a gathering
Suddenly, a call.

Suddenly, an ambulance
Suddenly, the lights
Suddenly, a heart stopped
Suddenly, the fright.

Suddenly, the ER
Suddenly, a code
Suddenly, deciding
Suddenly, you know.

Suddenly, the stillness
Suddenly, the tears
Suddenly, you were so far
Suddenly, so near.

AUGUST 1

Today is a day of
dreams lost,
taken from the world
as God watched—

    and cried.

August 1 (part 2)

Today the earth shook
and broke something beautiful,

   and darkness came

before the sun went down.

WHAT IS SACRED

I tore the bread
with my fingers.
    "Body of Christ,
    broken for you."

I sipped the wine
from the cup.
    "Blood of Christ,
    shed for you."

I held his broken body,
wiped the blood off of his face.
My stomach was left empty,
in my mouth, a bitter taste.

    Broken body. Shed blood.
    In the presence of the holy.

ORIGINAL BLESSING

by Jean Janzen

Child in the burning,
stopped heart in August,
this valley ripe
with peaches and heat.
What are the words
of original blessing?

Child become ashes,
the heaving and sobbing.
Body from body
into the blaze
of original blessing.

Child in the wind,
its current now lifting
into the arms
of original blessing.

Arms of the Maker,
arms of First Lover,
"Mine" the first word,
and the second, "Forever."

THE ONLY WORD (FOR DAVE)

I search the contacts
On my phone, hand
Shaking as I touch
The green call icon.

Afraid to say the words
I know will hurt,
My shaking voice a betrayal
Of something not right.

His first response, not a moment on,
A plea to say no more
About the news to come, as if
With that it might be undone—

"No."

His second cry
From deep within,
The spirit's groan for what he
Knew was my story's end—

"No!"

As I went on, spent and weak,
Each word flowed like the warm tears
Streaming down my cheeks,
The last a sob as he began to weep—

"No, no, no . . . . "

That was all he could say
With a heart now broken,
To protest, to pray,
Each "no" a word spoken

With the power to do nothing
And say everything
That needed to be said.

Destiny

I would rather be ashes than dust! I would rather that my spark should burn out in a brilliant blaze than it should be stifled by dry-rot. I would rather be a superb meteor, every atom of me in magnificent glow, than a sleepy and permanent planet. The function of man is to live, not to exist. I shall not waste my days trying to prolong them. I shall use my time.

—JACK LONDON

We held that box of bones
for the last time
and returned him to dust,
scattering his star stuff

to the places he
first carried those bones—
from the Sierra to the Pacific
and the Great Plains of Kansas,

now become a
shooting star whose
earthly glory burned out
in a brilliant blaze, exploding

into the cosmos—
every atom
a magnificent glow
in the universe,

a superb meteor,
now a spark
in the awakened planets
of our sleepy lives.

Inevitable?

Being born.
  Always a risk, however small.

Coxsackievirus (hand, foot, and mouth disease).
  Complications can lead to meningitis or encephalitis.

A pea stuck up your nose as a toddler.
  Not a real threat (blew it out through the other nostril).

Ran into the street chasing a ball or a squirrel.
  Like every child does, I suppose.

Buried under a towering pile of Labrador snow.
  Your brothers running inside for help.

Ran through a plate glass window.
  Multiple stitches from head to toe.

Stick to the head (more than once).
  Fantasy martial arts play in the back yard.

Fell into cold mountain stream.
  While on a family hike in the Rockies.

Nearly rolled the car off a dirt construction mound.
  Teetered on the edge of disaster.

Skateboard fall #1.
  Scraped up and bruised going downhill near the Rose Bowl.

Wrecked the pickup truck.
  Rear-ending another car in the rain.

Did it again (totaled this time).
 Nearly ended up beneath a flatbed trailer.

Broken collar bone.
 One of several football injuries.

Blowing shit up (What could go wrong?).
 Hearing loss and abrasions, as it turns out.

Another hiking fall.
 Down a steep power plant pipeline.

Encounter with the police.
 Chased by a helicopter, handcuffed on the street.

Knocked yourself out with a beer bottle.
 Showing how easily it would break (it didn't).

A hundred other things I don't know about.
 And the one I'll never forget.

II.

Birthday Wishes

I.
October Ten, your
Two hearts beat as one
On that day
You both came
Into the world.

II.
Tears of love and laughter
Along the way, as
Your hearts melded with mine—
You, me, and this boy,
Sorrow but a distant island
In a sea of unimagined joy.

III.
But this storm has come,
The sea now filled
With tears of sorrow
As wave upon wave
Came crashing down
Before twenty-one
Could come around.

IV.
Candles glow softly
On the face of memories,
Fading like wishes once made.
Now blown away, smoke trails
As I try to light them
Again and again.

V.
I'd take back every wish,
Return every gift,
Leave every memory behind
And close my eyes tightly
One more time

If that beautiful heart
Could beat again
      With mine.

LIFTED UP

You weren't even a toddler
but that didn't matter to me.
I put you on my back
in your snuggly carrier
past your bedtime
and your mother and I walked
down the street with you
to the tiny bookshop
where Rosa Parks
was going to be, to talk
about her book, *My Story*.
I wanted herstory
and others like it
to matter to you
like it did to me.

It was a chilly Pasadena evening
and we bundled you up,
leaving a small opening
for your little, cherub face.
Turning the corner from
the short walk
down Colorado Boulevard,
the line was long, the shop
not yet open. I knew right away
that we wouldn't get in,
not having Rosa's persistence.

Still, like the woman
who wanted just to touch the hem
of Jesus' garment, I wanted you
to see Rosa, this woman

of defiance and perseverance.
Perhaps, I thought, if you could
just look upon her face,
you and I and the world
could begin to be healed
of this "matter of blood."

As we turned and began
to walk away from the line,
I glanced down the alley
running alongside the store
and saw a dim, solitary glow
halfway down
the darkened passageway.
Taking your mother's hand,
we walked quickly
toward the opening of light—
a tic-tac-toe of security bars anchored
into the dark brown
cinder block wall.

I stood on my toes looking
through the dirty glass
to get a better view.
And there was Rosa, sitting—
as I imagined she had
so many years before—
tired and glad to be
resting at the back
of the store,
hands folded in her lap,
this time waiting patiently.

Without hesitation
I turned and loosened my arm
from the carrier strap,

bringing you around
in front of me, hurriedly removing
each chubby leg
from the warm blue canvas seat.
I lifted you face-forward
up to the window—
an act of faith, of dedication—
not knowing if you would see
the Woman Who Sat.

I wonder—in the throng
of book buyers and admirers,
did she look up,
sensing a power had gone
out from her, and did she turn
toward the window
and ask quietly to herself,
"Who looked upon my face?"

I held you there
long enough for Rosa
to touch us all,
and afterwards the three of us
retraced our steps back home,
blessed by a glimpse
into the past, lifted up
for the journey ahead.

Letting Go

To feed
  to clothe
    to clean,
      provide a roof overhead
        and shoes on your feet.

To hug
  to tuck in
    to tell stories to,
      change dirty diapers
        and walk you to school.

To wake
  to supervise
    to teach,
      (with actions and words)
        and give books to read.

To clown
  to learn from
    to tease,
      play and make laugh,
        crawl around on my knees.

To nurture
  to compliment
    to thank,
      discipline firmly
        and rarely to spank.

To forgive
　to talk with
　　to work alongside,
　　　tell you I'm proud
　　　　and let you decide.

To encourage
　to challenge
　　to help you achieve,
　　　always to love
　　　　unconditionally.

To praise
　to critique
　　to apologize to,
　　　be honest with
　　　　and motivate you.

To be there
　to cheer up
　　to talk about sex,
　　　to follow from one
　　　　event to the next.

To inspire
　to model
　　to advise,
　　　(like it or not)
　　　　and be by your side.

To question
　to challenge
　　to remind,
　　　advocate for
　　　　and carefully guide.

To support
　　to respect
　　　　to watch as you grow,
　　　　　　to bless and assure
　　　　　　　　and prepare you to go.

These things
　　I did,
　　　　well enough I suspect.
　　　　　　But the "what if" game
　　　　　　　　never lets me forget

the one job
　　I failed at
　　　　no dad can neglect,
　　　　　　most important of all:
　　　　　　　　just to protect.

And though
　　with each job
　　　　I prepared to let go
　　　　　　and thought that I had,
　　　　　　　　just how could I know

how sudden
　　how final
　　　　how hard it could be
　　　　　　when letting you go
　　　　　　　　came permanently?

MIGRAINES

I felt helpless
with you in my arms—
    too big to be held
    for any other reason,
rocking you gently,
whispering,
    "I'm here. I'm here."

But there was nothing
I could do except
    hold you and wish
    that I could
make it go away.
We both knew that I couldn't.
    Then, or now.

The room was dark because
the light hurt your eyes.
    But I could see your face,
    inches away from mine,
mouth wide open,
screaming silently.
    Is this what life is about?

I felt what you felt—
the pain in my heart
    an echo
    of what pounded
relentlessly
inside of you.
    Nothing I could do.

What I desperately, selflessly
wanted then to go away,
     I would gladly, selfishly
     welcome back—
even at
your expense.
     Just to hold you close again.

Brother Stuff (for Tim)

Crammed together
Shoulder-to-shoulder
In the photo booth—
Get ready!

One: that thing you do.
Two: your sexy look.
Three: Dad walking in on you!
Last one: brother stuff.

Immaculate Conception

Could Mary really have become pregnant
as a virgin? Welcome to Theology 101.

Of this, he dared to ask, on the radio no less:
"And did Mary have an orgasm when Jesus was conceived?"

I suspect that, with a bit more time, some other
questions would have come to mind.

What about God the Father—
did He have an orgasm too?

And did he call it "The Big Bang?"
Or is that just another theory?

Haiku (for Christine)

You gave us a gift
so great the debt alone is
a gift of its own

The Right Mix

The committee that meets to decide
on each year's recipient
of the Seth Dunn Memorial Fund Award
has been given the following
    formal guidelines
for making its selection:

> "A junior student who has made the most significant
> overall contribution to Bethel College community life.
> Primary consideration will be given to a student who
> identifies areas of needed change on campus, challenges
> others, and takes action that makes a difference in
> accordance with the stated ideals and values of the Bethel
> community."

In most cases, this will do.

However, in case the committee
is unable to determine which student
best meets those criteria, thus
finding itself unable to choose,
one of its members (who knew Seth well)
provides the following
    unofficial guideline
as a reminder of the true spirit of the award,
and I quote:

> "The person has to have the right mix of goodness and
> assholishness."

As with all informal rules,
this is the best criteria
to apply in selecting
the most deserving student
    for best honoring
the memory of Seth Dunn.

Congratulations!

CAREFREE

You were
launching into life
and I felt proud,
finally assured
that we were both
going to be

just fine.

Transport: An Anecdote

Seth Dunn, biology class presentation, 2010.

Lo, a semi-permeable membrane am I.
Constituents be forewarned! For I decideth thou fate.
If thou aspires to cross my threshold into the abyss of the cell
    membrane,
thou must understand the edicts and customs of mine own
    border.

Paramount, does thou necessitate diffusion?
For the expenditure of vigor on the part of mine shall equal none.
If thine art hydrophobic, as I aimed so near,
the atomies shall venture onward—
Hark! Knoweth thy passage shall be of much leisure,
for entrance to mine corse is through mine lipid bilayer.

Or dost thou seek trifling succor?
Denotement allows mine self to galvanize yonder transport
    conduits;
Engluttened thou shalt fadge in mind membrane.
So, provided thine conditions are correct,
permitted entrance you shall be!
Then aroint thee! Begone to thy journey's end.

Yea, lest thou art a slothful slug-abed,
against the concentration you wish to advance.
Off then, loggerhead,
know that my expenditure of ATP is seldom warranted,
exclusive of those dram of Potassium and Sodium.

Off to yonder ventures within the cell you shall go.
As for me, unpretentious and ever contemporaneous,
remain here I will, the gatekeeper,
my task enduring unbroken 'til my bereavement.

III.

What It Must Be Like

You can't imagine it
   because no one can.

There is no imagining—

only knowing
   or not knowing.

Misery's Shadow

Part of every misery is the misery's shadow or reflection: the fact
that you don't merely suffer but have to keep on thinking about the
fact that you suffer. I not only live each endless day in grief, but live
each day thinking about living each day in grief.

—C. S. LEWIS, *A GRIEF OBSERVED*

I think upon this broken heart,
   my suffering, my pain,
a constant, unrelenting part
   of every waking day.

But loss is not the only thing
   I suffer from each day;
its shadow—thinking endlessly
   of grief not going away.

It honors him, I tell myself,
   this sorrow that I feel,
a measure of my love for him,
pain making that love real.

At the bottom of an amber glass
   I find relief from pain,
its welcome numbness doesn't last,
   my grief comes back again.

Alone I sit with this despair
   where no one wants to stay,
some tell me, soon, that it will end,
   then quickly run away.

Others watch as I descend
    into the dark below;
Do I go down to get somewhere
    that they don't dare to go?

They need it to be better for
    themselves and are afraid
to think what might become of them
    if in this place they stayed.

I also fear what might be here,
    not part of my design,
that what once seemed a choice I made,
    is now no longer mine.

To flee despair, what might be lost—
    the memory of my son?
his smile? his laugh? his countenance?
    if love and pain are one?

For now I'll stay here godforsaken,
    alone where I must be,
this hell a shadow of my love,
    misery, my company.

THIN SPACE

nights thick and gray
as valley fog

i escape to be
alone

in my thoughts of you
headphones cancelling the noise

of your absence
i press play

and i'm free, music
bending time and space

the distance between us
overlapping, dissolving with

each lyric
each note

       electronica rap indie rock
       house edm trance folk

setting forth into the universe
catching glimpses

of one another
of the divine

where mystery is
cloaked in beauty

and the line between
heaven and earth

  collapses
     into
        love

Somewhere

Is rain always falling somewhere on the earth?

Somewhere raindrops scatter from a dense green canopy on high,
    falling like mist to the forest floor below.

Somewhere a cool monsoon gathers and rises, heavy clouds
    sweeping inland to drench hot and arid plains.

Somewhere a flash flood surges from distant showers,
    rushing into thirsty channels of wind-swept desert sand.

Somewhere thunder cracks and beckons a warm summer's rain
    as wide eyes watch from porches, huddled close.

And after the rain, as the sun breaks through parting clouds,
    droplets continue to fall toward the sodden but now-
    drying earth,

Leaving trails like tears, a reminder of the storm now past.

LAMENT FOR THOSE WITH NO NAME

After Laurie Halse Anderson

Lovers of the lost—
I name you,
though you are
without a name
because there is none
that speaks
to your pain
or this absence
now part of you
forever.

Lovers of the lost—
you already feel
the great nothingness
that comes with
losing those you love
and gives even them
a name: angel.

Lovers of the lost—
you shouted "No!"
outwardly or inwardly
and collapsed
because you
leaned on your
child when you
thought it was they
who leaned on you,
and wonder now

how you will
ever stand again.

Lovers of the lost—
you made arrangements
for those whom
you thought would
make arrangements
for you,
writing obituaries
and eulogies,
choosing plots
and scattering ashes
when you felt broken
into little pieces
and tossed
to the wind.

Lovers of the lost—
you cleaned rooms
or left them
untouched,
took years to sort
t-shirts for a quilt,
stitching together
the memories
of your child
and holding close
this comforter even
on the warmest of nights.

Lovers of the lost—
you saved keepsakes
and cards in boxes
you don't want to open,
that hold pain

from wounds
you cannot hide;
some day you will,
some day,
but that day
is not today.

Lovers of the lost—
you kept chairs
empty at holidays
and wished them
happy birthday,
lighting candles
even though your
grief kept you
from baking a cake
and what was once
a happy time
has become another day
just for tears.

Lovers of the lost—
I see you,
I will listen to you,
respect you,
honor your pain
and your fortitude,
your before
and your after,
your courage
and your hope
as you continue
with nothing more
than the strength
to take the next step
through this great adversity.

Lovers of the lost—
your angels
are everywhere
with you now,
an unceasing flame
burning with every
heartbeat
and breath you take;
hold them close
as you think of them,
recall their face,
say their name,
and yours.

For they are not far
and you are not alone.

INVOCATION

My heart leaps when you tell a story
   or say his name.
Please, don't fear that it might bring sadness
   not already there;
I have made a place for it inside,
   a part of me now unseen.
Hearing his name is not a reminder of loss
   (as if somehow forgotten) but a gift that says
I am not the only one
   who carries him with me—a reminder that
I do not keep him alive
   on my own.

A Thousand Times (for Laura)

Something you said
Reminded me of him.
I mentioned it once,
Or maybe twice.

But not the other
thousand times.

HEAVEN & HELL

It's not that I wish I believed it; I wish that it were true.

—BART EHRMAN

I wish there were
a heaven and hell
where I might burn
forever, tormented only
by my fate; perhaps
wishing that Lazarus
might cool my tongue
from beyond
the pearly gates.

Or, perhaps without
a hand or eye,
I would with all the saints
sing praises
in a sky of puffy clouds—
though lame,
reunited in paradise
with him again.

But this earth
is our heaven
and our hell, our
reward and torment
where we now dwell,
just or unjust,
our fate our own—
undetermined, unexpected,
uncertain, unknown.

And though a mystery—
assured, absurd,
no heaven or hell
to wish were so,
unknown, unfelt,
unseen, unheard,
this I do believe and know:
death has not
the final word.

But what does it mean
with paradise lost, if
what's done is done—
no more, no less,
no profit, no cost?

That this earth,
because of him,
has a little less hell,
a little more heaven;
more beauty and laughter
for us to behold,
more courage and hope
and love for our soul;

more life before death,
not age, but joy;
paradise found
in the form of a boy.

CREDO

Let go of god
and worry not
that god will
let go of you.

Let go of your
idea of god
that even god
does not have.

Let go of
the very
idea of god
itself

and all
the ways
it keeps you
from god

and you may
find yourself
closer to god
than ever.

Pilgrimage (for Johann)

The hill rises steeply
above the intersection where he fell,
but I no longer look up and demand
that it tells me why, or how.

I no longer insist that it
change the past; nor do I
replay those final moments
before it changed the future.

Instead, I look toward
the corner church and see
the sturdy Pride of Madeira, its cone-shaped
flowers deep with purple and life.

Pilgrims place sand dollars and clam shells
in a circle on the ground beneath its woody stems,
watched over by a Star Wars finger puppet
left by the red-headed boy

offering a sacrifice of his own.
Far away, they stand back-to-back
against a spinning silhouette,
the two melding into one.

In Memoriam

After Sherman Alexie

My son's name is Seth.

His name came from the Old Testament.

It would have been Hannah had he been born a girl.

His middle name is his mother's family name, as are his brother's.

My son's name is Seth.

His name means anointed, appointed, or placed, in Hebrew.

Seth was the third son of Adam and Eve, born after a long period of mourning the death of Abel, killed by Cain.

Eve considered Seth to be a replacement for her murdered son Abel, compensation.

We too associate Seth with mourning.

We have no replacement, no compensation.

My son's name is Seth.

Sometimes people would think it was Jeff.

We playfully called him Sether.

We yelled his name in anger.

We said his name with pride and joy.

We cursed his name (sometimes under our breath, sometimes not) in exasperation.

Mostly, we said his name with love and affection.

My son's name is Seth.

It seems odd to say a name so rarely after saying it thousands of times.

I have met other Seths and when I hear their name, I catch my breath.

Their name is not his name. It is close, but they are not him.

My son's name is Seth.

You could not hear his laugh without saying his name.

You could not see his face without saying his name.

Seth could not be known without his name.

My son's name is Seth.

Some people can no longer say his name.

Some people say his name to honor it, to honor him, and us.

I wonder how many times his name would have been said by now.

I wonder how many times his name would have been heard—by himself and others.

I wonder how long it would take to catch up if I started saying his name now?

My son's name is Seth.

There is a plaque with his name on it in the memorial garden of our church.

There is a plaque with his name on it at the place he used to work.

There is a stone with his name on it underneath a tree.

There is another stone with his name on it painted in Star Wars font, guarding his ashes atop a hill, unmoved like a Stormtrooper.

There is no grave or headstone anywhere with his name on it.

Let these words be a memorial for him.

Seth Bailey Dunn. Oct. 10, 1990—Aug. 1, 2011.

IV.

PTSD

The ring tone
startles my heart
with fear

and my imagination
runs wild
as I anxiously account

for the whereabouts
of what remains of my
hopes and dreams.

TORT

Profit from pain?
Turn loss into gain?
Alleviate a curse

Or just make it worse?
Calculating from birth
How much a life is worth.

Responsibility, liability—
Does it bring tranquility?
Perhaps just upward mobility.

No number I can reduce you to—
A million? A billion?
I'd give it up for you.

The World Continues to Spin

I sit at the stop light unaware that it has turned green,
oblivious to the horn behind me

      as the world continues to spin.

I roam the aisles of the store and into the checkout,
paying for my groceries without knowing the amount

      as the world continues to spin.

I stand in front of the class and begin to speak,
hearing familiar but distant words come out

      as the world continues to spin.

I wonder what my current state might get me out of—
a traffic ticket? a day of work? the rest of my life?

I fantasize about what it might get me into—
an argument? a fight? looking for the slightest slight

      as the world continues to spin.

I begin to notice that I am not alone. Like me,
others seem lost, distant, grieving, weary from the struggle

guarded and wanting a bit more space,
wounded and needing a bit more grace

      as the world continues to spin.

Sibling Rivalry

It is not of course the child's number in the order of successive births which influence his character, but the total situation into which he is born and lives, and the way in which he interprets it.

—ALFRED ADLER, MD

They jockeyed for position
as normal siblings do—
oldest, youngest, middle;
one, three, two.

When Adler said
it's not the number
but what the children do,
did he say what happens

when one becomes three,
or three becomes two?

Rearranged

Four framed images hang
in the bathroom, just so the wall isn't blank.
Our sons never took notice of them
or the platitudes they offered

to teen-aged boys and guests.
Peace. Love. Joy. Hope.
A curious place for inspiration.
Contemplation. Constipation.

One day, not long after he was gone,
I looked up and noticed Joy,
reversed and hanging upside down—
only one a trick of the mirror,

the other like a flag in distress,
out of place and conspicuous, rearranged
in a simple act of (re)decoration.
Desperation. A declaration

calling out incredulously—
Joy? What joy?
I had no inclination to straighten it out
(or the one who had changed it).

Why should anything be allowed
to remain unchanged? Soon
Faith too was hanging in doubt in this
barometric chamber of family emotions.

I occasionally checked back, noting that
Hope and Love remained intact.
And, eventually, all four were returned
to the way they were—

at least on those walls.

FULL DISCLOSURE

It's the kind of conversation
where you
see it coming—
Nice to meet you.
Work? Married?
Kids? (that's the one)

You'd think
a simple number
(three) would be easy.
But the number
leads to—
Boys? Girls? and then
names and ages
and eventually
the need for an explanation.

Or a lie.

Have I said two?
Yes. And fuck you.
I know what you're thinking
because I've thought it too:
How could you?

But I'm holding him closer
at that moment than you could
possibly know—
not letting go.

This small talk
leaves me wide open,
where an ordinary question
discloses a private answer,
the secret password
to who I am.

And I don't know yours.

Wrong Number

I dialed
the seven numbers
just to hear his voice

or this time see
if someone else
might answer

and tell me
what they've learned
about him

from all the other
unknown callers
like me.

PLATITUDES

In the face of suffering, our response must either be silence or the
word that is born of our tears.

—POPE FRANCIS

Your words
of assurance
offer no comfort to me
as I toss and turn
from the nightmare
of my grief.

Your outstretched hand
wipes away the tears
of your own distress
as you offer
an empty promise
I cannot imagine

and do not even want.
Instead, I long for
the presence of those
who sit and offer
nothing more
than silence and tears.

V.

A Tiny Love Story

Maybe we learn to love a person, say, first as object, and then as presence, and then as essence, and then as disclosure of the divine.

—LI-YOUNG LEE

Losing you
has led to
a kind of love
I never
knew
anything
about.

Rejection Letter

After Margaret Atwood

I assure you (he said)
that it did receive
careful attention

serious consideration
in-depth analysis
was processed as promised.

We feel that it
trends a bit toward
almost too relentless

in this particular focus
in this particular (he said) grief.
Possibly the poems are yet

too close to the loss
to really work as poems
a matter of what it takes

to transmute raw expressions
of feeling into poetry.
He said:

This may stir readers a bit too much.

A Beanie and a Cup of Tea
(Things They Wanted Us to Know)

"He showed up at my house with that silly beanie on his head.
The white Chihuahua we have has the great name of Rico. Seth
said, 'Rico suave.'"

"I will always think of Seth as synonymous with joy."

"Seth once borrowed my 1980's Spanx to wear for our dodgeball
game. He looked better in them than I did."

"Seth always made people laugh!"

"Seeing Seth walk across campus not really having a care in the
world. Always, always having a smile on his face."

"I spent hours upon hours discussing the zombie evacuation
plans with Seth. We spent so much time doing this that people
got pissed off and refused to be around us, but it didn't matter
because we were enjoying these ridiculous conversations so
much."

"Seth always had an air of mischief about him and was known for
'stealing' random things around the dorm."

"I always admired how he never hesitated to say hello to anyone
he passed on campus."

"Seth was so talented, and just made an impression on everyone
he met."

"Seth helped us with a prank during the first weekend of his junior year. It was an excessively childish prank but it's a memory I cherish because none of us involved could stop laughing."

"Seth gave amazing bear hugs. I am a grown man and Seth would squeeze the air out of me every time I saw him, whether I asked for it or not (mostly not). During the squeeze, he would also rub his facial hair on my face, making me uncomfortable. Strangely, I also felt very comfortable every time he did this to me."

"The first time I saw Seth he came sprinting into class, hair disheveled, beard unkempt, and the biggest smile and loudest laugh I've ever heard."

"Your son was full of joy and laughter and life."

"He was always willing to run around and climb trees that were impossible to climb."

"Seth's clever wit and pleasant demeanor made me happy every time I saw him."

"Seth was his own man."

"Seth was an incredibly talented actor and he made me feel like I was doing a good job even though my role was small."

"Every time I would pass Seth with a small group he would say, 'Hello gents' with a smile."

"I remember playing on Seth's dodgeball team. He always wore a Hawaiian shirt, he got counted out when the ball hit it."

"Seth saved my life. He helped me steer away from drugs and alcohol. All in all, he cared for me without having to. He was a light in my night and day."

"Seth touched everyone around him. He was a constant light on campus."

"Seth was a beautiful person who spread light, love, and laughter everywhere he went. He had an amazing gift of making every individual he came in contact with feel special, appreciated. He helped people find their value and worth as human beings."

"Every day was a good day with Seth, and it rubbed off on people."

"Seth was ridiculous, bawdy, and bombastic. He let me read raunchy romance novel excerpts on the radio show on Valentine's Day. Ken was running in and out of the booth telling us we went too far. But Seth just kept telling me to keep going. Seth was fucking great."

"I was a guest on Seth & Creigh's radio show one night. I was told the show would end with me playing a drum solo on Seth's face. I was reticent, to be sure, but when the time came I played his face. He was laughing hysterically with flushed cheeks and squinted eyes. It was wonderful."

"I'm not sure I ever saw him frown."

"Seth was a person who was joyful, sarcastic, funny, clever, enthusiastic, and engaged with the world. And I'm sorry that we never got to see what he would do when he found his path and found out what changes he wanted to make in the world we live in."

"The first time I met Seth he walked into my house unannounced and without knocking. I was about eight months pregnant and a little agitated. So I said, 'Who the hell are you walking into my house without knocking?' to which he replied, 'Where's Zach and who the hell are you?'"

"One time I fell asleep on his dorm's couch and when I woke up, he had made me a cup of tea, just for the heck of it. Not only was he one of the funniest, most sociable people I know, but he was also one of the kindest."

Thank you, friends, for these kind words that say so much about who Seth was, and is, to us all. We count them as a gift. Even the most remarkable story is a familiar one, though at times the magnitude of Seth's kindness and his significance to individuals and the Bethel community is still a surprise and a source of great pride and joy to us.

Let us not do Seth or our memories the injustice of pretending that he was perfect. None of us is. But he was perfectly Seth, and his outsize self has left a Seth-sized hole in each of us. Like these precious gifts, he has left us with memories of his joy, his smile, his laughter, and his love to fill it with.

FIVE MINUTES

This morning
when I woke,
five minutes went by
before I thought of you.

When the guilt and worry
of that moment passed,
I took a breath
and watched the sun come up.

Visible Mending

"Beautiful scars
for the loved but torn,"
the website says
about old garments
worn and tended
with yarning and darning,
each blemish
a story adorned with memories,
each repair
a bold and visible cover,
plain and lasting
for all to see.

Seams ripped,
cuffs snagged,
holes torn,
making visible
the work
to restore what's lost,
a garment mended
with each stitch and patch
lovingly placed and worn
as a badge to honor
and say,
I won't let go,
I will not throw
the past away.

Invisible Mending

Snags and tears,
cuts and burns,
moths and wear—
the warp and woof of life
leaving scars I care
for no one to see.

Painstaking work
for no one but me—
repairing, restoring
a way to re-weave
this well-worn fabric,
personal *kaketsugi*.

Making invisible
what seems beyond repair,
gently pulling
on what's still there,
the warp and weft
of what was threadbare.

Unraveled strands inside
now hidden on the outside,
giving new life
to this tapestry
hanging by a thread—
this garment of me.

3:33 A.M.

With thanks to Bruce Cockburn

Dreams of him suspend me
    within this unknown
    but familiar place
    where those left behind
and the departed embrace.
    Always giving me vertigo.

Dreams of him transport me
    from grief renewed
    to gratitude
    from hesitation
to "Again! How soon?"
    Setting my heart to burn.

Dreams of him leave me
    between doubt
    and possibility
    guide me through
this star-strewn space.
    Overflow my cup with grace.

Dreams of him transform me
    from disbelief
    to certainty
    from skeptic to believer
from shaman to fool.
    Waking this stumbler up to love.

The Waters (for Susan)

Poetry is the journal of a sea animal living on land,
wanting to fly in the air.

—CARL SANDBURG

The sea in which we frolicked,
Contented with its satisfying
Waters of joy, was my
Blessing of pups in a pod,
Ducks in a row, you swimming
By my side, together nestled
Among the reeds that calmed the surface,
The beyond unknown.

Then at once we found ourselves
Tossed up on this empty sand,
Far above the current where
The fragile reef has been undone
By the rushing tide
Of the river's endless flow.

Looking back, I steady myself
And grasp your hand, knowing
That we cannot return but wary
And uncertain of this unfamiliar land.

From here we've spent hours
Sitting together in silence, staring
Into the water or occupied
By something else,
Barely touching or not at all.
No need for words.

Some of those moments
Were spent in fear
That what was lost
Might come between us,
A rising tide pulling you or me
Back into the sea.

And then, a glint on the water's edge,
Wavy and surreal, a reflection
Of where we've been,
What we've lost. Together
We stand, ready to be free
From the sea and its past
As this fleeting vision calls us
Beyond this barren strand.

What shattered within each of us
And washed upon the shore
Is what remains, where we must now
Find beauty in the whole-but-imperfect
Brokenness of our fate, forever
Shared with one another,
Accepting the unacceptable,
The unimaginable now binding us
Together as we rise above
The waters of our grief.

Autumn's Return

The majestic red maples and burr oaks
cast their leafy shadows across
the gently sloping campus green,
branches swaying aimlessly in search of you.

We wander too, retracing your imagined steps
among the well-worn paths
that took you to Mojo's and Convo,
class and "creekers"—early and, mostly, late.

Walking in your footsteps beneath these trees
makes me feel like we have something in common
with them now, with all your friends,
known and unknown to us—

a quiet sense for what your absence will mean
as autumn comes and leaves begin to change,
laughing out loud with red and orange,
released to blanket the ground below.

Those who miss you take solace as we do
in knowing that this inevitable cycle of change
goes on unchanging—carrying us through this season,
comforted as we walk among these familiar friends.

Acknowledgments

I NEVER THOUGHT OR PLANNED to write a book of poetry. So I'm not being trite in saying that this collection would never have been possible if it weren't for so many people, most of whom will go unnamed here, though I am exceedingly grateful to all.

If there is any poetry within the pages of this book, it is because of Jean Janzen. You sat with me as a friend and mentor through the work of writing and grieving. Those were sacred moments of grace and healing. Thank you.

Thank you to Hope Nisly, Fran Martens Friesen, and Steve Penner for your gentle but critical reading of so many of these poems as part of our writing group. I cherish your love of words and your keen insight, so much of which comes from freely sharing your work with me. Our time together is one of the things I look most forward to each month.

Thanks to my university colleagues for their encouragement and support of my work, most notably Peter Smith and Marshall Johnston for their kind and generous recommendations in support of my sabbatical. Thank you, Ron Herms, for recognizing and affirming a personal project of passion, and to Fresno Pacific University for making space available for such endeavors.

I am undeservingly blessed to have a special group of people in my life who are both brilliant and among the kindest human beings on the planet. I am grateful to each of them not only for carefully reading my work and providing invaluable feedback, but for sitting with me, walking beside me, and listening to me for many hours—often just in silence—when that was what I needed most. Thank you, Christine Crouse-Dick, Laura Schmidt Roberts, Tim Neufeld, and Quentin Kinnison. You are more sisters and brothers to me than colleagues and friends.

Others affirmed this project when I was still unsure about it by reading one or many poems or providing me with an opportunity to share them with others. Thank you, David Augsburger, Cindy

Acknowledgments

Kinnison, Greg Stobbe, Dave Kleschold, Julia Baker Swann, Michael King, Jeff Gundy, and Elaine Enns. Thanks also to Matt Wimer and Emily Callihan at Wipf and Stock for your help in bringing this book to fruition, and to Jonathan Hill for your excellent care and assistance with typesetting.

Thank you, Eli and Isaac, for sharing with me that these poems were difficult—or too difficult—to read. I understand. And thank you for never giving up on me when it was so difficult for me to be the dad you needed. I see so much of your brother in each of you but love you for who you are on your own more than you could ever imagine.

Thank you, Susan. You read every poem through eyes filled with tears. You alone know and feel every word on every page as I do. You have been with me during and in between the writing, always. You make it possible to live with the unimaginable.

Thank you, Seth, for being with me every day.